THE HAPPY CHILD

12 Ways To Raise A Joyful & Contented Kid

Jojo Star Press

Dedication

To my dearest daughter Ava,

You are the heart and soul of this book, "THE HAPPY CHILD: 12 Ways To Raise A Joyful & Contented Kid." From the minute you entered my life, you radiated unending love, pleasure, and laughter. Every word on these pages is a result of your contagious joy and dazzling soul.

This book is dedicated to you with the utmost thanks and pride. You have imparted to me priceless knowledge of the genuine meaning of fulfillment and pleasure. Your unshakable happiness and capacity for delight in the little things have served as a continual reminder of the immense influence that a contented child can have on the world.

Thank you, my precious Ava, for being the inspiration behind "THE HAPPY CHILD." May your life always be filled with abundant happiness and endless joy.

With all my love,

PsyD. Jane Artwoord.

Table of Contents

Chapter XII: Emphasizing the Importance of Love and Connection

Introduction

I might be biased, but growing up in the 1990s was awesome. Things were a lot easier back then. We rode on bikes. Writing notes on paper was how we shared information with our friends. Finding out when the neighborhood game of release or tag began was our main worry. Life was easy.

Classic board games like Monopoly, Scrabble, and Chess were being played by groups of families and friends gathering around the table. Do you recall how these games fostered interpersonal communication and strategic thinking?

As a parent, I frequently catch myself thinking back on my own childhood experiences and comparing them with what today's kids are going through. In the 1990s, we often played outside, and our playground was the neighborhood.

We created inventive games that would keep us occupied for hours on end while also building forts, scaling trees, and other things.

It's simple to feel overwhelmed and unsure of the best methods to raise a pleasant and contented child as we navigate motherhood in this new era.

How can we combine utilizing technology with fostering interpersonal relationships? How can we support our kids in locating genuine joy in the middle of the dynamic social media, academic demands, and extracurricular commitments?

In "*The Happy Child: 12 Ways to Raise a Joyful and Contented Kid,*" we set out on a voyage of research and learning.

We will explore the essence of bringing up a happy kid in the 21st century by drawing on the timeless values that made our own childhoods memorable, as well as the revelations of contemporary research and professional guidance.

Let's learn how to make our homes a place where our kids can grow into their best selves, where there is laughter, love, and true satisfaction. In today's environment, raising a child comes with both joys and difficulties.

Chapter I: The Foundation of Joyful Parenting

The first step on the road to joyful parenting is to provide a safe, nurturing environment for our kids. Similar to how nourishing soil encourages the growth of a flowering plant, a child's emotional, social, and cognitive development is supported by a loving environment. The importance of giving our children a loving, supportive, and encouraging home will be discussed in this chapter.

The Power of Unconditional Love

Love is a language that is universal and cuts through all boundaries. It serves as the basis for a child's emotional stability and sense of security.

By fostering a close bond between parent and kid, unconditional love creates a secure environment where the child may freely express their feelings, thoughts, and dreams without worrying about being judged or rejected.

Children have a strong basis for developing self-esteem and confidence when their parents consistently demonstrate their love for them via their words, actions, and gestures.

A child who grows up in a loving family learns to love and cherish themselves, regardless of their accomplishments or flaws. As adolescents mature, they absorb this love, which serves as a foundation for their interpersonal interactions and worldview.

Nurturing Positive Parent-Child Relationships

Fostering a healthy parent-child connection is at the core of parenting, which is a journey that never stops changing. It takes persistence, comprehension, and open communication to develop a solid relationship with our kids.

The foundation for trust and collaboration is laid by a healthy parent-child connection, which makes it simpler to deal with the difficulties that come as our children mature.

Listening with Empathy

Understanding the feelings and needs hidden behind spoken words is part of listening, which goes beyond only hearing them. In order to establish a more meaningful connection with our children, it is essential to practice active and empathic listening.

They feel seen and heard when we sincerely listen to their stories, worries, and goals because we validate their experiences and feelings.

Communication as a Two-Way Street

The foundation of a healthy parent-child connection is excellent communication. It entails listening to our children's opinions and ideas as well as communicating our own views and expectations. Open communication promotes trust and makes it possible for mutual respect to grow.

Quality Time and Shared Experiences

Finding the time to spend entirely with our children in this fast-paced environment may seem difficult. Fortifying the link between parents and children, however, requires setting aside meaningful time for sharing experiences.

These shared experiences, whether it be a dinner, a game night, or just a stroll through the park, foster a sense of belonging and experience for a lifetime.

Cultivating Empathy and Emotional Intelligence

The capacity for empathy is the capacity to comprehend and experience another' emotions. It is a basic component of emotional intelligence, which entails skillfully identifying and controlling our emotions.

Our children get valuable life skills through having empathy and emotional intelligence developed, which contribute to their general happiness and well-being.

Modeling Empathy

The actions and attitudes of parents are models for children to follow. We may teach our children the virtue of empathy and understanding by demonstrating it in our daily encounters with others.

Emotional Literacy and Regulation

Finding healthy ways to express and control our emotions as well as identifying and comprehending them are all part of emotional intelligence. Children who are taught emotional literacy are better able to recognize and express their emotions, which prevents emotional repression and promotes a healthy emotional outlet.

Supporting Emotional Expression

We may foster an environment where our kids feel secure sharing their joys and sorrows by encouraging them to express their feelings honestly and freely. Even if we don't entirely comprehend what they're going through, we can still show our acceptance and support by validating their emotions.

Family Gratitude Jar - Encourage everyone in the family to record daily gratitudes in a gratitude jar that you will create. Share these notes aloud at meals or at the end of the day. This activity encourages positive psychology and respect for one another, which helps create a caring and encouraging environment.

Empathy Role-Play - Play role-playing games with your kid to help them develop empathy and comprehension. Take turns playing out various scenarios and feelings to help your youngster learn to put themselves in other people's shoes and think how they might feel. This fosters emotional intelligence and empathy.

Positive Affirmations Mirror Activity - Take turns speaking uplifting statements about yourself and your kid while you stand before a mirror with your youngster. Self-esteem is raised by participating in this exercise, which also emphasizes the value of positive self-talk.

Daily Hug and Heart-to-Heart - Spend a few minutes each day giving your child a special hug and having a heart-to-heart talk with them. Ask them about their day, check in with their feelings, and provide supportive and encouraging comments during this time.

The "Appreciation Sandwich" - Use the "appreciation sandwich" strategy for discussing problems or having family conversations. Start by complimenting your child on something they did right, then talk about the problem or struggle, and finish with another encouraging comment. This method addresses issues while preserving a friendly and encouraging environment.

Emotion Cards Game - Design emotion cards with varied facial expressions to reflect the various emotions. Shuffle the deck, then take turns choosing a card and discussing what may produce that emotion. By teaching kids how to identify and comprehend various emotions, this game promotes emotional intelligence.

Love Letters - To demonstrate their love and admiration for one another, family members should be encouraged to write each other love letters. When you want to connect and bond with each other, you may put these letters in a unique box and read them aloud.

Family Vision Board - Together, create a family vision board with images and text that reflect your common goals and objectives. Display it prominently in your house to serve as a constant reminder of your shared objectives and to create a warm and welcoming atmosphere.

Random Acts of Kindness Challenge - Encourage your family to perform random acts of kindness for one another and other people. Talk about how these actions affect everyone's feelings and how they help to create a more welcoming and compassionate environment.

"Walk in My Shoes" Activity - As a family, take turns recounting a trying circumstance you encountered today. After each individual has spoken, encourage the group to respond in a way that is encouraging and compassionate toward one another's experiences.

For further resources to build your kid's emotional intelligence and empathy, I recommend these workbooks created by me;

Self-Regulation Workbook for Kids Available on Amazon.

Emotional Intelligence Workbook for Kids Available on Amazon.

Chapter II: Fostering A Growth Mindset

Fostering a mindset of growth is a crucial pillar in the process of raising a happy and fulfilled child. A growth mindset is a conviction that skills and intellect can be improved through commitment, effort, and persistence.

Children who adopt this viewpoint develop resilience, motivation, and an openness to learning from both achievements and failures. In this chapter, we'll look at how fostering resilience, accepting failure, and a "can-do" mentality may help our kids develop a growth mindset.

The Power of Resilience and a Positive Attitude Towards Challenges

Challenges are a part of life, and how we respond to them affects our perspective and development. As parents, we have a significant influence on how our kids react to challenges.

Encouragement of resilience and the development of a positive outlook on difficulties equips people to overcome challenges with grit and optimism.

Teaching Problem-Solving Skills

Developing our kids' problem-solving abilities is one method to foster resilience. When confronted with difficulties, assisting them in breaking down issues into manageable steps enables them to tackle challenging circumstances with confidence.

A proactive mentality is encouraged by hammering home the point that every issue has a fix, enabling people to take on obstacles head-on.

Celebrating Effort and Persistence

Praise for effort and perseverance rather than concentrating just on results teaches our kids the value of commitment and hard work. Reminding them of their prior successes and the work they put in motivates them to keep moving forward when they are faced with challenges.

Embracing Mistakes as Opportunities for Learning and Growth

Teaching our children that making errors is not only normal but necessary for growth and development is imperative in a culture that frequently prioritizes perfection.

Their mindset changes from one of fear of failure to one of openness to experimentation when they accept mistakes as teaching opportunities.

Creating a Safe Environment

We must provide a secure setting where failures are viewed as stepping stones toward success in order to promote risk-taking and experimentation.

Children feel more comfortable pushing their boundaries and trying new things when they are certain that their errors will be accepted with compassion and support.

Shifting the Focus from Failure to Growth

We may encourage our kids to reframe their thinking so they don't view errors as failures. Encouragement comes from questions such, as "What did you learn from this experience?" and "How can you improve next time?" These questions help people shift their attention from the result to the process of learning and developing.

Promoting a "Can-Do" Attitude in Your Child

The confidence in one's capacity to overcome obstacles and achieve objectives is known as a "can-do" attitude. Children who are raised with this mindset are empowered to tackle things with confidence and passion because they are aware of their potential for success.

Setting Realistic Goals

Breaking down larger objectives into smaller, manageable stages makes them less overwhelming and more reachable, which motivates your kid to take action. Encouraging your child to set realistic and achievable goals creates a "can-do" mentality.

The "Challenge Chart" - Make a challenge chart where you and your child may write down the various tasks or objectives you wish to complete. Together, monitor your development and honor the efforts made, no matter the result. This activity promotes fortitude and a cheerful disposition toward difficulties.

"Mistakes are Opportunities" Discussion - Have frequent family talks regarding errors and failures, highlighting the fact that they are normal occurrences and excellent teaching opportunities. Give examples from your own life when errors resulted in the development and good things.

"I Can, I Will" Affirmations -Together with your youngster, start each day with "I can, I will" affirmations. Together, utter affirmations like "I can learn new things," "I will try my best," or "I can overcome challenges." The "can-do" mentality and strong self-belief are fostered by this activity.

Obstacle Course Adventure - Challenge your youngster to successfully complete an obstacle course you've set up in your living room or garden. Praise their perseverance and efforts, and exhort them to keep trying even if they encounter difficulties.

"Failure Celebration" Game - Play a "failure celebration" game to make failure a cause for celebration. Everyone applauds when someone makes a mistake or has a setback, and the person who encountered the failure gets to discuss what they learned from it.

"Growth Mindset Book Club" - Read books that stress the value of resilience and a development attitude. Talk about the characters' experiences, the difficulties they encountered, and how they accepted failure to learn from it.

"Changing the Narrative" Activity - By "changing the narrative," you may assist your child in reframing their thinking when they encounter a setback. Instruct them to replace any unfavorable self-talk with comments that are uplifting and empowering.

"Growth Mindset Journal" - Encourage your child to create a growth mindset journal in which they may record their experiences, difficulties, and key life lessons. This notebook acts as a reminder of their development and advancement.

"The Power of 'Yet'" - Don't be afraid to use the word "yet" in discussion. For instance, if your youngster says, "I can't do it," add the word "yet" to the end and respond, "You can't do it yet, but with practice, you will." This small change encourages a development mentality.

"Role Model Stories" - Share examples of successful people who overcame obstacles and disappointments on their path to success. Talk about how they adopted a development attitude and persevered in the face of challenges.

For further resources to build your kid's ability to take on tasks and complete tasks, I recommend this workbook created by me.

Executive Functioning Workbook for Kids Available on Amazon

Chapter III: The Power of Play and Creativity

Recognizing the transforming impact of play and creativity in our children's lives is crucial in the fast-paced, technologically-driven society in which we live.

The foundation of a child's holistic development is play, which is more than just a means to kill time. In this chapter, we'll look at the importance of unstructured playtime, the benefit of encouraging artistic expression, and the necessity of striking a balance between screen time and active and imaginative play.

Recognizing the Value of Unstructured Playtime

Free play, usually referred to as unstructured play, is an essential component of a child's development and well-being. It refers to a play that is kid-led and self-directed, where kids are free to explore, create, and make decisions without being constrained by anything outside of themselves. Numerous advantages of this kind of play establish the groundwork for a happy and comfortable childhood.

Fostering Imagination and Creativity

Unstructured play fosters a child's inventiveness and imagination. Children get the flexibility to create their own stories, investigate novel concepts, and solve problems in creative ways when they play with no set rules or goals. They may assume different roles via imaginative play, which promotes empathy and a better awareness of their surroundings.

Encouraging Artistic Exploration

Children are inspired to develop their artistic side when given access to art equipment and materials. Drawing, painting, sculpting, and creating are all activities that improve fine motor skills, raise self-esteem, and cultivate a sense of achievement.

Setting Screen Time Limits

Children learn that technology is simply one of many activities in their daily routine when clear and realistic screen time limitations are established. We can help children develop physically, emotionally, and socially by setting limits and encouraging them to engage in various types of play.

Encouraging Outdoor Play

Children can engage in physical exercise, sensory experiences, and a connection to nature through outdoor play. By encouraging outdoor play, you may help your children learn about the marvels of nature and develop awe and respect for their surroundings.

Promoting Playful Learning

Children's minds may be effectively engaged by fusing enjoyable learning activities with technology. Other types of play can be complemented with interactive educational applications and programs that encourage creativity, problem-solving, and critical thinking.

Engaging in Family Playtime

Playtime with the family not only improves parent-child relationships but also promotes active and imaginative play. Togetherness while engaging in games, sports, or artistic pursuits fosters lifelong memories and emphasizes the importance of non-screen engagement.

"Playtime Planner"- Make a weekly schedule of playtimes as a family, setting up designated times for unstructured play, creative play, and craft time. This activity assists in putting play and creativity first in your child's everyday routine.

"Playdate Scavenger Hunt" - Set up a playdate scavenger hunt in your yard or a nearby park to promote free play and discovery. Give the kids a list of things to find, and then let their adventures be led by their imaginations.

"Imagination Station" - A designated "Imagination Station" in your house will allow your kid to play imaginatively with open-ended toys, costumes, and props. Encourage them to come up with their own scenarios and stories.

"Art Gallery Showcase" - Create a family art gallery where you may display your kid's creations. They are proud to show off their creations and talk about the inspirations and feelings that went into each one.

"Storytelling Circle" - Take turns sharing inventive tales as a family in a warm circle. Use image cards, or narrative starters, or just let your imagination run wild.

"Tech-Free Time" - Designate certain times of the day when no technology is allowed so that the family may play active games or do creative things together. This activity aids in striking a balance between screen time and other types of play.

"DIY Craft Challenge" - Give your youngster a package of unrelated materials and a DIY craft challenge where they must use those components to create something original. Ingenuity and resourcefulness are fostered by this exercise.

"Nature Exploration" - Join your child on a trek or nature walk, and encourage them to gather pebbles, leaves, and other natural objects. Use these supplies to create crafts or include them in fantasy play.

"Puppet Show" - Assist your kid in making puppets out of socks or paper bags and performing a puppet show. Through this practice, they may develop their imaginative storytelling abilities and promote self-expression.

"Playtime Swap" - Set up a playtime swap with other parents in which your child visits a friend's home and vice versa. This promotes social bonds and gives kids the chance to play in various contexts.

"Creative Sensory Play" - Make sensory bins containing a variety of materials, like grains, beans, or sand, along with toys and equipment for exploration. Playing with your senses helps to spark imagination and creativity.

For further resources to build your kid's playability, I recommend this coloring book created by me.

The Bullying Ends With You: Anti-Bullying Coloring Book For Kids Available on Amazon

Chapter IV: Cultivating Gratitude and Appreciation

Cultivating gratitude and appreciation is a transforming discipline that may bring happiness, satisfaction, and a profound feeling of fulfillment into our lives in a world full of distractions and unending needs.

Giving our kids this spirit of thankfulness as parents is a priceless gift that will influence how they view the world and how they interact with others.

This chapter will discuss the value of instilling in kids a feeling of gratitude for life's small pleasures, fostering compassion, and teaching them to appreciate their blessings.

Teaching Your Child to Count Their Blessings and Practice Gratitude

The art of gratitude is the recognition and appreciation of all the wonderful things and gifts in our lives, no matter how great or tiny. By encouraging them to express appreciation and recognize their blessings, we help our kids develop a positive outlook that they may use to overcome obstacles.

Gratitude Journal

Encourage your kid to start a thankfulness diary in which they may record things each day for which they are grateful. They are able to concentrate on the good and consider how abundant their lives are thanks to this activity.

Gratitude Rituals

Make expressing gratitude a family habit by sharing a few things you are thankful for before bed or during meals. Inculcating the habit of seeing and appreciating goodness in daily life is the goal of this practice.

Thank You Notes

Encourage your child to write thank-you letters or notes as a way of teaching them the value of appreciation. A meaningful thank-you card helps to build appreciation, whether it is for gifts, deeds of kindness, or assistance received.

Acts of Kindness and Generosity

In addition to helping others, acts of kindness and giving help our children develop empathy and compassion. These behaviors encourage generosity and gratitude in the heart.

Mindful Eating

With mindful eating, you may help your kid appreciate the nutrients that food provides by teaching them to relish each bite. By doing this, they learn to appreciate the nutrition and tastes in their food.

Sunrise or Sunset Appreciation

Watch the dawn or sunset together by getting up early or staying up late. Talk about the wonder of these natural occurrences and how they serve as a reminder of life's brief but priceless moments.

Thankful Tree - You may help your kid create a visual picture of their blessings by asking them to write something they are thankful for on a leaf-shaped piece of paper each day and tie it to the tree.

Gratitude Rock - Together, you and your kid may choose and embellish a particular rock. When your child feels thankful, they can hold the gratitude rock and say "thank you" aloud by placing it somewhere where it can be seen.

Gratitude Board Game - Together with your kid, make a game with a thankfulness theme. Use a dice and game pieces, and as players go over the board, they are required to give an act of gratitude that corresponds to the color or number on the dice.

Kindness Coupons - By having them perform deeds of kindness for family members, you may help your child create kindness coupons. Breakfast in bed or helping with chores are two examples. These vouchers are available for use at any time by family members.

Chapter V: Building Healthy Habits and Self-Care

The development of good habits and the promotion of self-care are crucial elements of a kid's overall well-being with the aim of raising a cheerful and pleased child.

In order to cultivate a healthy lifestyle, it is important to prioritize physical health via balanced eating and frequent exercise, teach relaxation skills and stress reduction, and promote appropriate sleep. In this chapter, we'll look at how these behaviors support children's joy, resiliency, and overall feeling of satisfaction.

Prioritizing Physical Health Through Balanced Nutrition and Regular Exercise

The basis of a healthy and prosperous existence is a body that is well-nourished. We provide our kids the best chance to acquire healthy habits that will improve their physical and emotional well-being by placing a high priority on a balanced diet and frequent exercise.

Healthy Snack Options

Allow your kid to pick from a range of healthy snack alternatives. To promote healthy eating, keep a variety of whole-grain snacks, nuts, fruits, and veggies at your fingertips.

Cooking Together

Include your child in the cooking and food preparation process. This not only imparts useful culinary knowledge but also fosters a love of healthful, home-cooked food.

Encouraging a Variety of Exercises

Encourage your child to try various sports, dances, yoga, or swimming as physical activities. This encourages a lifetime love of fitness while also assisting them in finding things they enjoy.

Teaching Relaxation Techniques and Stress Management

Stress and worry may harm kids in today's fast-paced society. They get the ability to deal with difficulties and resiliently traverse the ups and downs of life by learning relaxation techniques and stress management.

Deep Breathing Exercises

With your kid, engage in deep breathing techniques to promote relaxation and stress management. Simple exercises like "belly breathing" might help you relax and find your center.

Mindfulness and Meditation

Practices of mindfulness and meditation should be taught to your child. Stress reduction and self-awareness can be improved by participating in guided meditation sessions or mindful hobbies like coloring or listening to peaceful music.

Encouraging Adequate Sleep for a Well-Rested Child

For a child to develop physically and mentally, adequate sleep is essential. We can make sure that our kids are well-rested and prepared to take on each day with vigor and joy by modeling appropriate sleeping habits.

Consistent Bedtime Routine

Create a regular nighttime routine with relaxing activities like reading a book or taking a warm bath. The body receives a signal from this practice that it is time to relax and get ready for bed.

Creating a Sleep-Friendly Environment

Make sure your child has a sleeping environment that encourages sound sleep. To encourage better sleep, keep the room dark, quiet, and chilly.

Healthy Meal Planning - Participate with your child in the creation of a healthy food plan. Together, come up with a menu for the coming week that includes a range of healthful meals and discusses their advantages.

Nutritional Scavenger Hunt - Set up a scavenger hunt in the market or the grocery store. Give your child a list of foods that are healthy to locate and explain to them why each one is essential to good health.

Exercise Challenge - Together with your kid, create a fitness challenge. Make a chart where kids may record the number of jumping jacks, skipping or other exercises they perform each day. Provide incentives for succeeding in the task.

Breathing Buddies - By utilizing "breathing buddies," you may teach your child how to relax. Place a stuffed animal on their tummy and have them lie down. Then, while they are breathing slowly and deeply, have them watch the buddy gently rise and fall.

Stress-Free Storytelling - Prior to going to sleep, organize a stress-free storytelling activity. Invoke your child's creativity to create a tale in which they are the hero who faces difficulties head-on and overcomes them with grace and fortitude.

Bedtime Yoga - Include relaxing yoga postures for bedtime in your child's nightly routine. To encourage a calm transition to sleep, lead them through moderate stretches and relaxation techniques.

Chapter VI: Nurturing a Love for Learning

Instilling a passion for learning in our children is one of the most priceless gifts we can give them since education is a voyage of discovery and progress.

Fostering a lifetime love of learning requires establishing a positive and stimulating learning environment at home, developing a curiosity-driven approach to education, and recognizing academic success while embracing a passion for learning that extends beyond grades.

In this chapter, we'll dive into these habits and consider how they affect our kids' zeal for learning, intellectual curiosity, and never-ending quest for information.

Creating a Supportive and Engaging Learning Environment at Home

The basis for a love of learning starts at home, where parents are crucial in influencing their kids' views toward education. Children may explore, ask questions, and cultivate a sincere enthusiasm for learning in an environment that is encouraging and stimulating.

Designated Learning Spaces

A comfortable reading nook, an art corner, or a study room can all be designated learning areas at home. These areas convey the value of learning and provide learners with a feeling of control over the learning process.

Encouraging Open Communication

Encourage open dialogue about difficulties and learning opportunities. In order to provide a secure environment for intellectual inquiry, encourage your kid to share their ideas, inquiries, and discoveries.

Reading Together

Regularly read to your kid while exploring a range of themes and genres. Demonstrate a passion for reading and participate in debates about the books and concepts you encounter.

Learning Beyond the Classroom

Include chances for experiential learning outside of the classroom. To pique interest and broaden their horizons, people should visit museums, go to educational events, and go on outdoor adventures.

Instilling a Curiosity-Driven Approach to Education

The motivation for meaningful learning experiences is curiosity. We provide our kids with the tools they need to ask questions, look for solutions, and see learning as an exciting adventure by fostering a curiosity-driven approach to education.

Encouraging Questioning

Even if you don't know the answers, accept and encourage your child's inquiries. Foster an inquiry- and critical-thinking-based mindset by discussing these issues together.

Project-Based Learning

Participate in project-based learning activities that let your kid explore interest-related subjects. These assignments offer chances for independent study and the pursuit of information out of curiosity.

Diverse Measures of Success

Place a strong emphasis on many success indicators that go beyond academics, such as creativity, problem-solving, and flexibility. Honor the times when your youngster applied what they learned to actual circumstances.

Science Experiments - Use common home objects to do basic scientific experiments with your child. Encourage children to create projections, pose questions, and then track the outcomes to develop an enthusiasm for inquiry-based education.

Learning Quests - Set up scavenger hunts or learning quests that require your child to research or learn about particular topics. Use hints and interactive features to create an engaging and fun experience.

Reading Challenges - Set reading goals for your child and offer prizes depending on the number of books they finish or the amount of time they spend reading. Incentivize them to explore other genres and acknowledge their efforts.

Show and Tell - Establish a weekly "Show and Tell" session so that your child may share something new or exciting they have learned. This practice fosters their love of learning and increases their self-assurance while speaking in front of an audience.

Educational Games Night - Set aside a night to play puzzles and instructive games. Play board games with strategy, thought, and problem-solving components to make learning fun for the whole family.

Personal Projects - Encourage your child to pursue interest-based personal projects. These projects, which can involve making a model, writing a story, or producing art, encourage creativity and a passion for independent study.

Virtual Field Trips - Go on virtual field trips to museums, monuments, or other tourist destinations all over the world. To learn more about other cultures and history, use internet tools to visit these locations as a group.

Learning Reflections - Encourage your child to think back on their daily learning. Encourage a habit of active learning and self-awareness by asking open-ended questions to elicit their views and observations.

Celebrating Effort - Regardless of grades or results, recognize and applaud your child's efforts and advancement throughout their educational path. Highlight the importance of lifelong learning and development as opposed to merely academic success.

Chapter VII: Developing Social Skills

Strong social skills are the threads that weave enduring friendships, meaningful relationships, and a strong feeling of belonging into the tapestry of a happy and comfortable childhood.

The ability to successfully navigate social situations, comprehend the feelings of others, and communicate with others is a social skill that children must develop as part of their evolution.

This chapter will discuss how to develop wholesome friendships and pleasant social interactions, how to instill empathy and concern for others' feelings, how to promote efficient communication, and how to resolve conflicts, all of which will pave the way for our kids to develop enduring connections.

Fostering Healthy Friendships and Positive Social Interactions

Friendships are essential to a child's social development because they give them company, support, and a feeling of community. We provide our kids with a solid basis for forming fulfilling relationships by encouraging healthy friendships and encouraging positive social interactions.

Encouraging Inclusive Play

Encourage inclusive play where kids with various interests and experiences may interact and take part in activities that promote understanding and friendship.

Modeling Positive Social Behavior

In your relationships with others, serve as a good social role model. Be a role model for your child by acting with respect, compassion, and inclusion in all of your interactions.

Promoting Teamwork

Encourage children to participate in cooperative games and activities where they will learn the importance of collaboration, compromise, and working toward shared objectives.

Practicing Sharing and Turn-Taking

Teach your kid the value of sharing and turning over while they're playing with others. They gain an understanding of the idea of collaboration and reciprocity as a result.

Teaching Empathy and Compassion for Others' Feelings

The foundation for deep connections with other people is empathy and compassion. Our children develop a deep sense of understanding and kindness as a result of our efforts to teach them empathy and compassion for the feelings of others.

Active Listening

Teach your child the skill of active listening, which requires them to focus only on the words and feelings of others without interrupting. Deeper relationships and empathy are fostered by this exercise.

Identifying Emotions

Help your kid notice and name their own emotions so that they may use this knowledge to recognize and comprehend the emotions of others.

I-Statements

Encourage your child to utilize "I-statements" to calmly convey their wants and feelings. "I feel upset when..." or "I need help with..." are two examples.

Conflict Resolution Strategies

Give your child advice on how to resolve conflicts by compromising, taking a pause to relax, and coming up with win-win solutions.

Role-Playing Communication Scenarios

Your child may experiment with numerous methods to express oneself in various settings by role-playing communication scenarios.

Friendship Bracelets - While making friendship bracelets, have a conversation about what makes a good friend. Discuss the value of being helpful in friendships, compassion, and empathy.

Feelings Charades - Play the game "Feelings Charades" with your child, in which they play out various emotions while you try to identify them. Take advantage of the chance to talk about empathy and comprehending others' emotions.

Emotion Guessing Game - Play a game of "guess the emotion" in which you or your child acts out a certain feeling and the other person tries to identify it. Discuss the significance of acknowledging and respecting others' feelings.

Sharing Circle - Create a sharing circle for your child, their siblings, and their friends. Turn-taking encourages open communication and empathy among the group members as each person shares something uplifting or significant.

Conflict Resolution Chart - Together with your child, make a chart showing how to settle disputes amicably. Refer to this during arguments and urge your child to take the initiative in settling disputes.

For further resources to build your kid's interpersonal/social skills, I recommend this workbook created by me;

Interpersonal skills workbook for kids Available on Amazon

Chapter VIII: Mindful Parenting

Parenting with mindfulness in the chaos of modern life may be a transformational and empowering way to raise a child who is happy and fulfilled.

Being completely present, paying attention, and acting without bias while interacting with our kids is a key component of mindful parenting. We can lessen stress, strengthen our relationships with our kids, and set a good example for them by adding mindfulness to our parenting journey.

In this chapter, we'll examine the benefits of mindful parenting, including how it may help us be present with our kids and manage stress, as well as how it can help us discipline them and solve problems.

Practicing Mindfulness to Reduce Stress and Be Present with Your Child

The practice of mindfulness is being completely present in the here and now with an unprejudiced awareness. By focusing on the present moment and letting go of fears and distractions, parents can be truly present with their children and appreciate the beauty of each priceless moment.

Mindful Morning Routine

Include a thoughtful morning ritual that involves a minute of silence, making intentions, or being grateful. Invite your child to begin the day with you in mindfulness.

Mindful Language and Communication

Set an example for others by speaking politely and quietly, especially in difficult circumstances. Teach your child how to speak thoughtfully, empathetically, and actively.

Using Mindful Approaches to Discipline and Problem-Solving

Discipline and problem-solving may be changed by mindfulness from reactive to deliberate and compassionate methods. By reacting thoughtfully, we provide a secure and encouraging atmosphere for our kids to study and develop.

The Pause Button

Use the "pause button" approach whenever you feel irritated or angry. Before replying to your child, take a moment to take a deep breath and count to 10. This will give you time to answer thoughtfully rather than quickly.

Mindful Time-Outs

Introduce thoughtful time-outs in place of typical time-outs, allowing you and your kid to take a few minutes to cool off and gather your thoughts before addressing the situation.

Mindful Breathing - Together with your kid, practice mindful breathing. Together, choose a comfortable seat, close your eyes, and inhale slowly and deeply. To assist in keeping the mind present, count your breaths.

Mindful Art - Together, make conscious art by coloring, painting, or making something. Keeping your attention on the process rather than the outcome will encourage creativity and awareness.

Mindful Emotions Check-In - Persuade your kid to monitor their feelings throughout the day. To assist them in carefully identifying and expressing their emotions, use an emotion wheel or a feelings chart.

Mindful Parent-Child Communication - Set a good example for your child by paying attention to what they are saying without interrupting or passing judgment. Encourage open and honest conversation by validating their feelings and responding gently.

Chapter IX: Encouraging Independence and Decision-Making

To nurture and mentor our children as they grow into autonomous, successful adults is one of our main responsibilities as parents.

It is crucial for their growth and development to promote independence and decision-making since it gives them the freedom to make their own decisions, gain experience from mistakes, and develop self-confidence.

 In this chapter, we'll look at how crucial it is to give kids a certain amount of autonomy and independence, encourage them to make their own decisions and build their self-esteem via these experiences.

Allowing Age-Appropriate Autonomy and Freedom

Children naturally show curiosity and a desire to investigate their surroundings from a young age. They are given the opportunity to develop their personality and identify their interests when given autonomy and freedom that are age-appropriate.

Supporting Your Child in Making Their Own Choices and Learning from Consequences

Even at an early age, letting kids make their own decisions helps them learn how to make decisions and accept responsibility for their actions. This method's key component is learning from the results

Offering Options

Give your child options within a certain framework. For instance, allow them to select which of two wholesome snack alternatives to have or which book to read before bed.

Learning from Mistakes

Instead of being excessively judgmental when your child makes a decision that results in a less-than-ideal outcome, encourage them to learn from their errors. Promote resiliency and creative problem-solving.

Natural Consequences

Allow natural events to play out as they should. For instance, rather than saving your child from misery when they forget their raincoat and get wet in the rain, use the situation as a chance to teach them something.

Building Self-Confidence Through Decision-Making Experiences

Making decisions provides kids with priceless chances to develop self-assurance and faith in their talents. They get a sense of autonomy and confidence in their talents when they make decisions and deal with the results.

Affirming Independence

Recognize and applaud your kid for making autonomous choices to boost their self-confidence. Honor their efforts and the decision-making process that went into them.

Responsibility Chart - Create a chart of responsibilities with duties appropriate for your child's age. Give children the freedom to select their daily tasks and keep track of their accomplishments to help them develop a feeling of independence and ownership.

"I Can Do It" List - Help your kid make an "I Can Do It" list of chores that they are confidently capable of completing on their own. As they advance, recognize their successes and add additional assignments.

Choice-Based Meals - Give your child a voice in the selection and preparation of meals. Give them a menu of wholesome choices and let them decide what they want to eat for particular meals.

"Consequence or Reward" Game - Play a game with your child in which they must balance the advantages and disadvantages of several options. Together, discuss the potential outcomes to help them learn to think about the effects of their choices.

"What If" Scenarios - Your kid should be exposed to a variety of "what if" questions, such as "What if you forget your homework at home?" and "What if your friend wants to play a different game?" Encourage them to come up with a list of potential answers.

Parent-Child Role Reversal - Change roles with your child from time to time, letting them make decisions for you as necessary. This activity encourages empathy and comprehension of the difficulties in making decisions.

"Two Truths and a Lie" - Play the game "Two Truths and a Lie" with your kid, in which you each tell two truths and one falsehood. To encourage critical thinking and observation, your kid must determine which of two statements is false.

Self-Assessment Exercises - With your kid, do self-evaluation activities where they identify their advantages and places for improvement. Encourage them to make choices that are in line with their desires by helping them develop goals.

Chapter X: Embracing Nature and Outdoors

Reconnecting with nature and the outdoors is a potent approach to raising a happy and satisfied child in the fast-paced, technologically-driven society we live in.

In addition to improving physical health, spending time in nature also improves mental health, generates awe, and strengthens our bond with the natural world.

In this chapter, we'll look at the many advantages of embracing nature and the great outdoors, participating in outdoor activities that improve health and connection to the environment, and providing opportunities for exploring and appreciating the natural world in order to foster a peaceful relationship with the planet.

Exploring the Benefits of Spending Time in Nature

Children and adults alike may benefit from nature, which is an endless source of wonder, beauty, and inspiration. Children who spend time in nature benefit greatly from it on a variety of levels, including their physical, mental, and emotional health.

Enhanced Physical Health

Playing and exploring outside promotes physical exercise, which benefits kids' motor abilities, coordination, and general fitness. Natural sunshine exposure also encourages the development of vital minerals like Vitamin D.

Boosted Creativity and Imagination

The marvels of nature inspire imaginative thinking and creativity. Children are frequently inspired by their experiences outside to create stories, games, and artwork.

Enhanced Cognitive Development

A rich environment for learning and exploration may be found in nature. Children explore the natural environment while using problem-solving, observational skills, and critical thinking.

Gardening and Planting

Get your kid involved in gardening tasks, such as seed planting and plant care. A sense of obligation and respect for the natural environment is fostered by this experience.

Camping and Stargazing

Consider going camping or scheduling stargazing sessions so that you and your child can appreciate the wonders of the night sky. This encounter cultivates awe and amazement for the cosmos.

Beach and Water Play

Take your child on excursions to the beach or other bodies of water nearby so they may enjoy the relaxing effects of the ocean and participate in beach activities.

Wildlife Observation

Engage in nature observation, such as noticing butterflies, birds, or other animals in their natural environments.

Environmental Stewardship

Teach your kid the value of Earth protection and environmental responsibility. Participate in community clean-up programs and eco-friendly activities.

Cloud Watching - Together, view the clouds while lying in a green space. Encourage your kid to use their imagination to spot creatures or forms in the clouds to inspire creativity and a feeling of wonder.

Nature Photography - Give your kid a camera or a smartphone, and let them use it to capture the beauty they see in the outdoors. When they look back at the images, kids can talk about what they found most fascinating or intriguing.

Picnic in the Park - In a local park or natural area, organize a picnic. Enjoy dinner outside with your loved ones while taking the time to explore the local wildlife and flowers.

Nature Music and Dance - Make music and dance activities inspired by nature. Dance wildly outside while singing tunes about the trees, animals, or weather.

Chapter XI: Navigating Challenges and Difficult Emotions

There are countless events in life, both enjoyable and difficult. Our responsibility as parents is to stand by them as they navigate life's ups and downs, assisting them in controlling their stress, anxiety, and depressive moods, and promoting honest dialogue about their emotions.

Giving kids coping mechanisms for trying circumstances enables them to develop self-awareness, emotional intelligence, and resilience.

We will discuss the significance of helping your kid manage stress, anxiety, and unpleasant emotions, encouraging open conversation about feelings, and aiding them in creating coping mechanisms that will benefit them throughout their life in this chapter.

Assisting Your Child in Managing Stress, Anxiety, and Negative Emotions

Children may experience tension, anxiety, and other unpleasant feelings as a result of the obstacles that life often brings. In order to aid them in navigating these emotions, it is crucial for parents to create a supportive and understanding atmosphere for their children.

Mindfulness for Emotional Regulation

Encourage emotional control techniques such as mindfulness. Children that are conscious of their emotions may recognize and understand such emotions.

Validating Emotions

Encourage your kid to express a spectrum of emotions by validating their feelings and reassuring them that this is normal. Do not minimize or ignore their feelings since this might impede their emotional development.

Feelings Journal

Encourage your kid to keep a feelings journal in which they may express their emotions via writing or drawing. They are able to digest their emotions and see patterns thanks to this exercise.

Emotion-Focused Activities

With your kid, take part in activities that are centered on emotions, such as reading books that examine emotions or playing games that promote emotional expressiveness.

Helping Your Child Develop Coping Strategies for Challenging Situations

Children that are resilient are more capable of facing difficulties with strength and adaptation. Giving your child coping mechanisms will give them the tools they need to deal with challenging circumstances.

Encouraging Healthy Outlets

Encourage your kid to use constructive outlets for tension and challenging feelings, such as exercise, artistic expression, or time spent in nature.

Seeking Support

Let your kid know that it's OK to ask for assistance from dependable adults, such as their parents, teachers, or counselors when they need assistance overcoming difficult circumstances.

Worry Box - With your kid, make a worry box. Have them put their anxieties on pieces of paper and deposit them in the box whenever they feel worried or concerned. Set aside certain periods for you and your partner to talk about and resolve these issues.

Feelings Collage - Have your child use magazine cutouts or illustrations that symbolize various emotions to make a collage of their feelings. Encourage them to discuss the significance of each feeling for them.

Feelings Check-In - Check-ins on your child's feelings on a daily basis. As you inquire about their feelings, urge them to be honest and judgment-free in sharing them.

Coping Strategy Board Game - Make a board game that includes coping mechanisms for difficult emotions. Play the dice and talk about various tactics that may be applied in various circumstances.

Emotion Drawing - Ask your child to illustrate how certain emotions feel to them. They may express their emotions more openly and externally thanks to this artistic activity.

Chapter XII: Emphasizing the Importance of Love and Connection

A happy and fulfilled childhood has love and connection at its core. The happiness and well-being of our children are built on the rock of our love as parents.

In order to develop a caring and connected connection with our children, it is crucial to prioritize quality time, establish family ties via shared experiences and traditions, and express unwavering love and support.

In this chapter, we'll examine the significant relevance of highlighting the value of connection and love in order to forge enduring ties and treasured experiences that will enhance our children's lives and influence their futures.

Strengthening Family Bonds Through Shared Experiences and Traditions

Family ties are strengthened and enduring memories are made when shared experiences and customs are observed. These common experiences weave together our children's formative years.

Holiday and Seasonal Traditions

Accept the seasonal and holiday customs that are particularly meaningful to your family. These customs provide a sense of joy and continuity among generations.

Expressing Love and Affection

Regularly express your care and love for your child. Hugs, kisses, and words of encouragement are straightforward signs of unfailing support and gratitude.

Encouragement and Positive Reinforcement

Support your child's efforts and accomplishments by giving them encouragement and showing your faith in their potential.

Family Meeting - Hold frequent family gatherings to talk about future plans, celebrate wins, and discuss any issues. Open communication and a sense of community are encouraged by this approach.